To

_____

CONGRATULATIONS! You did it!

From

_____

Date

_____

GRADUATE'S
CELEBRATION
BOOK OF WIT & WISDOM

COMPILED BY
ANNETTE LAPLACA

HAROLD SHAW PUBLISHERS, WHEATON, ILLINOIS

Compiled by Annette LaPlaca
Cover by David LaPlaca

ISBN 0-87788-814-0

Library of Congress Cataloging-in-Publication Data

The graduate's celebration book of wit and wisdom / compiled by Annette LaPlaca.
    p.   cm.
  Rev. ed. of: It came from my senior yearbook. 1992.
  ISBN 0-87788-814-0
  1. Conduct of life—Quotations, maxims, etc. I. LaPlaca, Annette Heinrich, 1964-   . II. Title: It came from my senior yearbook.
PN6084.C556I85 1996
082—dc20
                                        95-53696
                                           CIP

05   04   03   02   01   00   99   98

10   9   8   7   6   5   4   3   2

WHAT'S INSIDE

Moving On

Hanging On

Moving Out

MOVING ON

Congratulations!

Congratulations! Give yourself a pat on the back—graduation is an achievement to be proud of. Take time to enjoy the sweet taste of success.

Graduation is a ceremony that marks the end of study and the beginning of education.

Evan Esar, Esar's Comic Dictionary

We do not know who we are until we see what we can do.

Martha Grimes, Writer's Handbook, *in* Reader's Digest

No man ever reached to excellence in any one art or profession without having passed through the slow and painful process of study and preparation.

Horace

Education is discipline for the adventure of life.

Alfred North Whitehead

The test of a truly educated man is what he is, and what he thinks, and what his mind absorbs, or dreams, or creates, when he is alone.

Donald K. David

The object of education is to prepare the young to educate themselves throughout their lives.

Robert Maynard Hutchins

Love of learning is seldom unrequited.

Arnold H. Glasow

Education is the ability to listen to almost anything without losing your temper or your self-confidence.

Robert Frost

Genius is one per cent inspiration, and ninety-nine per cent perspiration.

Thomas Edison

Human knowledge is an island in a vast sea of the unknown.

Sir Isaac Newton

Education is a companion which no misfortune can decrease, no crime destroy, no enemy alienate, no despotism enslave; at home a friend, abroad an introduction, in solitude a solace, in society an ornament.

Jo Petty, Apples of Gold

Man's reach is always greater than his grasp, his achievements never equal his aspiration, his successes never equal his attempts, his answers never equal his questions. Such is life.

Dan C. Shannon

Success is faithfulness. . . . Success, then, comes when we faithfully study God's Word and faithfully obey it, applying what we understand to all areas of our lives under the direction of the Holy Spirit.

Kent and Barbara Hughes, Liberating Ministry

We must continually use the measure of our obedience to the guidelines of His Word as the real—and only—standard of our "success," not some more supposedly tangible or glamorous scale.

Charles Colson, Who Speaks for God?

Knowledge puffs up, but love builds up. The man who thinks he knows something does not yet know as he ought to know. But the man who loves God is known by God.

1 Corinthians 8:1-3

He who merits praise he never receives is better off than he who receives praise he never merits.

Keith L. Brooks, The Cream Book: Sentence Sermons

The educated man is one who has finally discovered that there are some questions to which nobody has answers.

Unknown

Every man has two educations—that which is given to him, and the other, that which he gives to himself. Of the two kinds, the latter is by far the more valuable. Indeed, all that is most worthy in a man, he must work out and conquer for himself.

Jean Paul Richter

If you have knowledge, let others light their candles by it.

Thomas Fuller

Perfect wisdom has four parts: wisdom, the principle of doing things right; justice, the principle of doing things equally in public and private; fortitude, the principle of not fleeing danger, but meeting it; and temperance, the principle of subduing desires, and living moderately.

Plato

If a man be endued with a generous mind, this is the best kind of nobility.

Seneca

It is not what we read, but what we remember, that makes us learned. It is not what we intend, but what we do, that makes us useful. It is not a few faint wishes, but a lifelong struggle, that makes us valiant.

Henry Ward Beecher

The worst use that can be made of success is to boast of it.

Arthur Helps

It isn't what you know but what you are willing to learn.

Cliff Schimmels, T-shirt Wisdom for the Graduate

I am sufficiently proud of my knowing something to be modest about my not knowing everything.

Vladimir Nabokov

The greatest ignorance is being proud of learning.

Unknown

But as for you, continue in what you have learned and become convinced of, because you know those from whom you learned it, and how from infancy you have known the holy Scriptures, which are able to make you wise for salvation through faith in Christ Jesus. All Scripture is God-breathed and is useful for teaching, rebuking, correcting and training in righteousness, so that the man of God may be thoroughly equipped for every good work.

2 Timothy 3:14-17

It is the work that God does through us that counts, not what we do for Him. All that our Lord heeds in a man's life is the relationship of worth to his Father.

Oswald Chambers, My Utmost for His Highest

The secret of success is a secret to many people.

Evan Esar, Esar's Comic Dictionary

Next in importance to freedom and justice is education, without which neither freedom nor justice can be permanently maintained.

James A. Garfield

He who has no inclination to learn more will be very apt to think that he knows enough.

A. Powell

Knowledge humbleth the great man, astonishes the common man, puffeth up the little man.

Keith L. Brooks, The Cream Book: Sentence Sermons

In the Christian life there are many promotions in spiritual growth, but there is no graduation.

T. J. Bach

Knowledge comes but wisdom lingers.

Alfred Lord Tennyson

Real success is more of an inward feeling than an outward show.

Unknown

Thought and learning are of small value unless translated into action.

Wang Ming

If at first you don't succeed, you have plenty of company.

Eldon Pedersen

Without experience one gains no wisdom.

Chinese proverb

Success comes from wide-awake days rather than sleepless nights.

Unknown

It is nonsense to talk of the college years as only a preparation for life.
They are part of life.

Paul Swain Havens

Wisdom is the scar tissue of intelligence.

Gene Gleason

Changing Directions

Graduation is a crossroads place in life. From here you'll go on to new challenges, new experiences. Exciting changes lie ahead!

"Forget the former things;
do not dwell on the past.
See, I am doing a new thing!"

Isaiah 43:18-19

Two roads diverged in a wood, and I—
I took the one less traveled by,
And that has made all the difference.

Robert Frost, "The Road Not Taken"

Change, like sunshine, can be a friend or a foe, a blessing or a curse, a dawn or a dusk.

William Arthur Ward

It will do no good to get on the right track if you then go in the wrong direction.

Evan Esar, Esar's Comic Dictionary

Change is the law of life and growth.

C. B. Eavey, 2500 Sentence Sermons

Stand at the crossroads and look; ask for the ancient paths, ask where the good way is, and walk in it, and you will find rest for your souls.

Jeremiah 6:16

We live in a crazy world and the only way to see it is to stand permanently on your head.

G. K. Chesterton

Spring is a promise
in the closed fist
of a long winter

Luci Shaw, "Faith," Postcard from the Shore

Change is the only constant thing in the universe.

Unknown

You have made known to me the path of life;
you will fill me with joy in your presence,
with eternal pleasures at your right hand.

Psalm 16:11

The Father comes near to take our hand and lead us on our way.

Mrs. Charles E. Cowman, Streams in the Desert

Jesus tells us that there can be no religion without adventure, and that
God can find no use for the shut mind.

William Barclay, The Gospel of Matthew, *on the parable of the talents*

The only way to get anywhere is to start from where you are.

William Lee

Dare to trust Him; dare to follow Him!

F. B. Meyer

WAIT

These are
the good
old days.
Just wait
and see.

Steve Turner, Up-to-Date

A good beginning is likely to mean a good ending.

Unknown

Lord, the newness of this day
Calls me to an untried way:
Let me gladly take the road,
Give me strength to bear my load,
Thou my guide and helper be—
I will travel through with Thee.

Henry van Dyke

How often we look upon God as our last and feeblest resource! We go to Him because we have nowhere else to go. And then we learn that the storms of life have driven us, not upon the rocks, but into the desired haven.

George MacDonald

Even if you're on the right track, you'll be run over if you sit still.

Unknown

Ideals are like stars. You will never succeed in touching them with your hands; but, like the seafaring man on the desert of waters, you choose them as your guide, and following them, reach your destination.

Carl Schurz

Don't think you are necessarily on the right road just because it is a well-beaten path.

Unknown

Making Decisions

Part of moving out in new directions is making decisions about things like career and relationships. Your day-to-day choices in these big questions will shape much of your life.

Choices are the hinges of destiny.

Edwin Markham

Trust in the LORD with all your heart
and lean not on your own understanding;
in all your ways acknowledge him,
and he will make your paths straight.

Proverbs 3:5-6

Whether you turn to the right or to the left, your ears will hear a voice behind you, saying, "This is the way, walk in it."

Isaiah 30:21

What would Jesus do?

Charles Sheldon, In His Steps

O Thou, who are the God no less of those who know thee not than of those who know thee well, be present with us at the times of choosing when time stands still and all that lies behind and all that lies ahead are caught up in the mystery of a moment.

Frederick Buechner, The Hungering Dark

Destiny is not a matter of chance, it is a matter of choice.

Unknown

Great minds have purposes; others have wishes.

Washington Irving

He who deliberates fully before taking a step will spend his entire life on one leg.

Chinese proverb

Not to decide is to decide.

Unknown

Every day we choose good or evil, right or wrong, holiness or sin, God or Satan.

C. B. Eavey, 2500 Sentence Sermons

Commit to the LORD whatever you do,
and your plans will succeed.

Proverbs 16:3

I thought
I was losing
my mind.
It was only
my imagination.

David Porter, "Suburbia Poem"

The greatest mistake you can make is to be continually fearing that you'll make one.

Elbert Hubbard

The strongest pain of growth lies in human choice.

George Eliot

A little uncertainty is good for everyone.

Henry Kissinger

Be transformed by the renewing of your mind. Then you will be able to test and approve what God's will is—his good, pleasing and perfect will.

Romans 12:2-3

In all decisions, the believer should humbly submit, in advance, to the outworking of God's sovereign will as it touches each decision.

Garry Friesen, Decision-Making and the Will of God

I will instruct you and teach you in the way you should go.

Psalm 32:8

To every man there openeth
A High Way, and a Low.
And every man decideth
The way his soul should go.

John Oxenham

If we are ever in doubt what to do, it is a good rule to ask ourselves what we shall wish on the morrow that we had done.

Lord Avebury

Living is a form of not being sure, not knowing what next or how. . . . We may be wrong, but we take leap after leap in the dark.

Agnes De Mille

Free will is not the liberty to do whatever one likes, but the power of doing whatever one sees ought to be done, even in the very face of otherwise overwhelming impulse. There lies freedom, indeed.

George MacDonald

We know what happens to people who stay in the middle of the road. They get run over.

Aneurin Bevan

I don't know the key to success, but the key to failure is trying to please everybody.

Bill Cosby

It does not take much strength to do things, but it requires great strength to decide on what to do.

Elbert Hubbard

It is not in life's chances but in life's choices that happiness comes to the heart of the individual.

C. B. Eavey, 2500 Sentence Sermons

Take courage when you have a tough decision to make. Someone who cares deeply for you already knows what he wants you to do. He takes delight in having fellowship with you and wants the very circumstances you face to draw you closer to him.

John White, The Fight

Let me be acutely attuned to Your Word, so that each decision I have to make will be in Your will, almighty God.

Billy Graham, Day by Day

Once to every man and nation comes the moment to decide,
In the strife of Truth and Falsehood, for the good or evil side.

J. R. Lowell

HANGING ON

Keeping the Faith

Your acceptance of salvation and trust in the Lord form a foundation of faith. Build confidently on this foundation—God keeps his promises (see Matthew 7:24).

I believe in Christianity as I believe the sun has risen, not only because I see it but because by it I see everything else.

C. S. Lewis

Faith means believing what is incredible, or it is no virtue at all. Hope means hoping when things are hopeless, or it is no virtue at all. And charity means pardoning what is unpardonable, or it is no virtue at all.

G. K. Chesterton, Heretics

Faith is to believe what we do not see. The reward of this faith is to see what we believe.

St. Augustine

Faith is being sure of what we hope for and certain of what we do not see.

Hebrews 11:1

Faith is not contrary to reason, but rather "reason grown courageous."

Sherwood Eddy

Faith is saying "Amen" to God.

Merv Rosell

Doubt isn't the opposite of faith; it is an element of faith.

Paul Tillich

Faith is the confidence that God's Word is true and the conviction that acting upon that Word will bring his blessing.

Robert C. Savage, Pocket Quips

Faith expects from God what is beyond expectation.

Unknown

Faith is necessary in *everything*.

J.B. Stoney

Faith is dependence on God. And this God-dependence only begins when self-dependence ends.

James McConkey

The highest pinnacle of the spiritual life is not joy in unbroken sunshine but absolute and undoubting trust in the love of God.

A. W. Thorold

Faith is being able to see with your heart what you cannot see with your eyes.

Robert C. Savage, Pocket Quips

The beginning of anxiety is the end of faith, and the beginning of true faith is the end of anxiety.

George Müller

Faith, walking in the dark with God, only prays Him to clasp its hand more closely.

Phillips Brooks

We have no more faith at any time than we have in the hour of trial. . . .
Fair-weather faith is no faith.

Charles H. Spurgeon

"In repentance and rest is your salvation, in quietness and trust is your
strength."

Isaiah 30:15

Faith is at the core of practical Christianity. Your Christian life began
when you began to believe. It has grown and will grow as faith widens
the channel along which grace flows to you. No aspect of your Christian
life is of greater importance.

John White, The Fight

God delights to increase the faith of His Children.

George Müller

Never try to arouse faith from within. You cannot stir up faith from the
depths of your heart. Leave your heart, and look into the face of Christ.

Andrew Murray

Doubt sees the obstacles; Faith sees the way.

Robert C. Savage, Pocket Quips

Faith comes from hearing the message, and the message is heard through the word of Christ.

Romans 10:17

Faith is just believing what God says he will do.
He will never fail us; His promises are true.
If we but believe Him, His children we become.
Faith is just believing this wondrous thing is done.

Children's song

It is not the greatness of my faith that moves mountains, but my faith in the greatness of God.

Unknown

When you get all wrinkled with care and worry, it's time for a *faith* lift.
C. B. Eavey, 2500 Sentence Sermons

Without faith it is impossible to please God, because anyone who comes to him must believe that he exists and that he rewards those who earnestly seek him.

Hebrews 11:6

'Tis so sweet to trust in Jesus,
Just to take Him at His word,
Just to rest upon His promise,
Just to know, "Thus saith the Lord."

Louisa M. R. Stead, "Tis So Sweet to Trust in Jesus"

Faith by itself, if it is not accompanied by action, is dead. . . . Show me your faith without deeds, and I will show you my faith by what I do.

James 2:17-18

If the Sun and Moon should doubt, They'd immediately go out.

William Blake

Faith is the soul's venture; it ventures all on Christ.

Unknown

Living in the Light

In this fast-paced, multimedia, hyperactive world, make it your number-one goal to love and serve your Savior. Seeking the abundant life Jesus promised means keeping in step with the Spirit (see John 10:10; Galatians 5:25).

Being confident of this, that he who began a good work in you will carry it on to completion until the day of Christ Jesus.

Philippians 1:6

May I run the race before me,
Strong and brave to face the foe,
Looking only unto Jesus
As I onward go.

Kate B. Wilkinson, "May the Mind of Christ My Savior"

One can never consent to creep when one feels an impulse to soar.

Helen Keller

Whatsoever weakens your reason, impairs the tenderness of your conscience, obscures your sense of God, or takes off the relish of spiritual things—whatsoever increases the authority of your body over your mind—that thing, to you, is sin.

Susanna Wesley

Do you not know that in a race all the runners run, but only one gets the prize? Run in such a way as to get the prize.

1 Corinthians 9:24

The soul that has once been waked, or stung, or uplifted by the desire of God, will inevitably (I think) awake to the fear of losing Him.

C. S. Lewis, Letters to Malcolm

I had far rather walk, as I do, in daily terror of eternity, than feel that this was only a children's game in which all the contestants would get equally worthless prizes in the end.

T. S. Eliot

True religion is the life we live, not the creed we profess.

J. F. Wright

For our light and momentary troubles are achieving for us an eternal glory that far outweighs them all. So we fix our eyes not on what is seen, but on what is unseen. For what is seen is temporary, but what is unseen is eternal.

2 Corinthians 4:17-18

The grand essentials to happiness in this life are something to do, something to love, and something to hope for.

Joseph Addison

The life of a man is a thing of potential beauty and dignity. . . . To live is good.

Unknown

Dost thou love life? Then waste not time; for time is the stuff that life is made of.

Benjamin Franklin

Sooner or later a man, if he is wise, discovers that life is a mixture of good days and bad, victory and defeat, give and take.

Unknown

Life is no brief candle to me. It is a sort of splendid torch which I am permitted to hold for the moment, and I want to make it burn as brightly as possible before handing it on to future generations.

George Bernard Shaw

We make a living by what we get, but we make a life by what we give.

Herbert V. Prochnow

It takes the whole of life to learn how to live.

Jo Petty, Apples of Gold

Jesus said to her, "I am the resurrection and the life. He who believes in me will live, even though he dies; and whoever lives and believes in me will never die."

John 11:25-26

A mighty fortress is our God,
A bulwark never failing.
Our helper, he, amid the flood
of mortal ills prevailing.

Martin Luther

Courage is grace under pressure.

Ernest Hemingway

We should concentrate on living within today. Then better tomorrows will inevitably follow.

Dale Carnegie

And the days are not full enough
And the nights are not full enough
And life slips by like a field mouse
Not shaking the grass.

Ezra Pound

Life—a little gleam of time between two eternities.

Thomas Carlyle

Give your life to God; He can do more with it than you can!

Dwight L. Moody

The Bible is God's road map.

Kenyon Palmer

God is always whispering to us, only we do not hear, because of the noise, hurry, and distraction which life causes as it rushes on.

F. W. Faber

The Christian ideal has not been tried and found wanting, it has been found difficult and left untried.

G. K. Chesterton

One can never pay in gratitude; one can only pay "in kind" somewhere else in life.

Anne Morrow Lindbergh

The real art of living is beginning where you are.

Unknown

To be patient in little things, to be tolerant in large affairs, to be happy in the midst of petty cares and monotonies, that is wisdom.

Joseph Fort Newton

To laugh often and love much

To win the respect of intelligent persons and the affection of children

To earn the approbation of honest critics and endure the betrayal of
  false friends

To appreciate beauty

To find the best in others

To give one's self

To leave the world a bit better, whether by a healthy child, a garden
patch
  or a redeemed social condition

To have played and laughed with enthusiasm and sung with exultation

To know even one life has breathed easier because you have lived—

This is to have succeeded.

Ralph Waldo Emerson

Each new day is an opportunity to start all over again . . . to cleanse our
minds and hearts anew and to clarify our vision.

Jo Petty, Apples of Gold

Putting Something In

It's easy to sit back and enjoy the blessings of life, but it's exciting to get out there and put something excellent, worthwhile, and true into the world—something unique only you can contribute.

That best portion of a good man's life—his little, nameless, unremembered acts of kindness and of love.

William Wordsworth

Seek always to do good somewhere. You must give some time to your fellow man. For remember, you don't live in a world all your own.

Albert Schweitzer

Expect great things from God. Attempt great things for God.

William Carey

Service is love in working clothes.

Keith L. Brooks, The Cream Book: Sentence Sermons

The world is before you, and you need not take it or leave it as it was when you came in.

James Baldwin

Never put off till tomorrow what you can do today.

Thomas Jefferson, Ben Franklin

PUT SOMETHING IN

Draw a crazy picture
Write a nutty poem,
Sing a mumble-gumble song,
Whistle through your comb.
Do a loony-goony dance,
'Cross the kitchen floor,
Put something silly in the world
That ain't been there before.

Shel Silverstein, A Light in the Attic

Life is like a game of tennis. The player who serves well seldom loses!

Robert C. Savage, Pocket Quips

Our will, done in our own strength, is humanism. Christ's will, done in our own strength, is religion. And his will, done by his power, is the abundant life.

Lloyd John Ogilvie

Small deeds done are better than great deeds planned.

Peter Marshall

To accomplish great things, we must not only act but also dream, not only plan but also believe.

Anatole France

The man who removes a mountain begins by carrying away small stones.

Chinese proverb

The world is moved not only by the mighty shoves of the heroes but also by the aggregate of the tiny pushes of each honest worker.

Helen Keller

It is only when we forget ourselves that we do things that are remembered.

Unknown

A man's true wealth is the good he does in this world.

Mohammed

"Who is a wise man and endued with knowledge among you? Let him shew out of a good conversation his works with meekness of wisdom."

James 3:13, KJV

With this kind of wisdom and knowledge, we may enter upon our chosen field of service and there find satisfaction and blessing, together with the tranquility of one who is subordinated to the yoke of Jesus Christ.

Hudson T. Armerding, A Word to the Wise

A Christian man is the most free lord of all, and subject to none; a Christian man is the most dutiful servant of all, and subject to everyone.

Martin Luther

Wherever there is a human being, there is an opportunity for kindness.

Seneca

Trust in God and *do* something.

Mary Lyon

Lost time is never found again.

Benjamin Franklin

The smallest good deed is better than the grandest intention.

Unknown

Not unless we fill our existence with an aim do we make it life.

Reichel

Our heavenly Father never gives us too much to do. . . . He knows what He wants from each of us, and there is plenty of time in His day for things essential to His plan.

Charles Shedd, Time for All Things

A man can do only what he can do. But if he does that each day, he can sleep at night and do it again the next day.

Albert Schweitzer

There never was a bad man but had ability for good service.

Edmund Burke

The best place to find a helping hand is at the end of your arm.

Elmer Leterman

They who have learned the way to live,
  Plant wisely, though they may not reap;
And this is well, since what we give
  Is all that we may hope to keep.

Margaret E. Bruner

I love the word impossible.

Ann Kiemel

The only gift is a portion of thyself.

Ralph Waldo Emerson

If good and godly men stand aloof from moral and societal obligations in matters civic or spiritual, social or educational, their dereliction of duty creates a vacuum to be filled by the ambitious and unprincipled.

V. Raymond Edman, Great Sermons of the Twentieth Century

Once we see the world and ourselves for what we are, we can help. Once we understand ourselves we begin to operate not from a posture of anger but of compassion and concern. We look at the world not with bitter frowns but with extended hands. We realize that the lights are out and a lot of people are stumbling in the darkness. So we light candles.

Max Lucado, No Wonder They Call Him the Savior

Do good with what thou hast, or it will do thee no good.

William Penn

Holiness is religious principle put into action. . . . It is faith gone to work. It is love coined into conduct; devotion helping human suffering, and going up in intercession to the great source of all good.

F. D. Huntington

We never know how high we are
Till we are called to rise;
And then, if we are true to plan,
Our statures touch the skies.

Emily Dickinson

It is better to busy oneself about the smallest thing in the world than to treat a half-hour as worthless.

Goethe

Give what you have. To some one it may be better than you dare to think.

Henry Wadsworth Longfellow

Never be lacking in zeal, but keep your spiritual fervor, serving the Lord.

Romans 12:11

We cannot do everything at once, but we can do something at once.

Calvin Coolidge

Far and away the best prize that life offers is the chance to work hard at work worth doing.

Theodore Roosevelt

That which we persist in doing becomes easier for us to do, not that the nature of the thing itself is changed, but that our power to do is increased.

Ralph Waldo Emerson

It is possible to be so active in the service of Christ as to forget to love him. . . . Christ can do without your works; what he wants is you. Yet if he really has you, he will have all your works.

P. T. Forsyth

Action springs not from thought, but from a readiness for responsibility.

Dietrich Bonhoeffer, Letters and Papers from Prison

Individuality is the salt of common life. . . . Be yourself if you would serve others.

Henry Van Dyke

I shall pass this way but once; if, therefore, there be any kindness I can show, or any good thing I can do to my fellow human beings, let me do it now; let me not defer nor neglect it, for I shall pass this way but once.

Abraham Lincoln

Staying on the Bright Side

Life gets stressful; pressures of all kinds can stretch you to your very limits. During times like those, it's important to invest some time in laughter. Seek the joy of the Lord, and the "bright side" of your circumstances eventually will appear.

Laff every time you pheel tickled, and laff once in a while enyhow.

Josh Billings

Laughter is the shortest distance between two people.

Victor Borge

Humor is emotional chaos remembered in tranquility.

James Thurber

Wit has truth in it; wisecracking is simply calisthenics with words.

Dorothy Parker

A little nonsense now and then
Is relished by the wisest men.

Anonymous

Laughter is the sensation of feeling good all over, and showing it principally in one spot.

Josh Billings

Laugh and the world laughs with you,
Weep and you weep alone,
For the sad old earth must borrow its mirth,
But has trouble enough of its own.

Ella Wheeler Wilcox

He who laughs, lasts.

Mary Pettibone Poole

I am never more tickled than when I laugh at myself.

Mark Twain

Laughter is the music of the soul.

C. B. Eavey, 2500 Sentence Sermons

Let a smile be your umbrella—and you'll get a mouthful of rain!

Unknown

Let us be determined to be happy; make the most of the blessings that come to us; look on the bright side of everything. Cheerfulness is not always spontaneous. . . . One who can carry a smiling face through a world where there are so many troubled hearts may unconsciously be a public benefactor; for "the merry heart doeth good like a medicine," and not alone to its possessor.

M. P. Wells

Enjoy yourself. It is later than you think.

Chinese proverb

It is a poor heart that never rejoices.

Anne Fremantle

Those who do not know how to weep do not know how to laugh either.

Golda Meir

The cheerful heart has a continual feast.

Proverbs 15:15

Grief melts away
Like snow in May,
As if there were no such cold thing.

George Herbert, "The Flower"

A smile is the lighting system of the face and the heating system of the heart.

Robert C. Savage, Pocket Quips

Happiness is like a pair of eyeglasses correcting your spiritual vision.

Lloyd Morris

The surest way to be miserable is to have the leisure to wonder whether or not you are happy.

George Bernard Shaw

Happiness is a warm puppy.

Charles Schultz

Laughter is real medicine. It has optimistic vitamins in it. It revives like oxygen. It restores failing morale. I have proved for myself the "cleansing power of laughter."

Gelett Burgess, "On Laughter"

Laughter is the best medicine.

Reader's Digest

A cheerful heart is good medicine.

Proverbs 17:22

Life is short, and we never have too much time for gladdening the hearts of those who are traveling the dark way with us. Oh, be swift to love! Make haste to be kind!

Henri Amiel

Most folks are about as happy as they make up their minds to be.

Abraham Lincoln

The world is like a mirror, reflecting what you do; and if your face is smiling, it smiles right back at you.

Unknown

God weeps with us so that we may one day laugh with him.

Jurgen Mottmann

No one is exempt from talking nonsense; the mistake is to do it solemnly.

Michael Montaigne

HAPPY THOUGHT

The world is so full of a number of things,
I'm sure we should all be as happy as kings.

Robert Louis Stevenson

It is enough that you and I,
    Whatever be our girth,
Shake a fist at fret and gloom,
    And gird the day with mirth.

Father Jerome

The happiness in your life depends on the character of your thoughts.

Marcus Aurelius

Finally, brothers, whatever is true, whatever is noble, whatever is right, whatever is pure, whatever is lovely, whatever is admirable—if anything is excellent or praiseworthy—think about such things.

Philippians 4:8

'Tis easy enough to be pleasant,
When life flows along like a song;
But the man worth while is the one who will smile
When everything goes dead wrong.

Ella Wheeler Wilcox

Much may be known of a man by what excites his laughter.

Goethe

All people smile in the same language.

Unknown

Happiness is a thing to be practiced—like a violin.

Unknown

ETERNITY

He who binds to himself a joy
Does the winged life destroy;
But he who kisses the joy as it flies
Lives in eternity's sun rise.

William Blake

If you can't crown yourself with laurels, you can at least wreathe your
face in smiles.

Unknown

A laugh can be a powerful thing.

Roger Rabbit

Be happy, young man, while you are young,
and let your heart give you joy in the days of your youth.

Ecclesiastes 11:9

Smile, once in a while,
   'Twill make your heart seem lighter.
Smile, once in a while,
   'Twill make your pathway brighter.
Life's a mirror, if we smile
   Smiles come back to greet us;
If we're frowning all the while
   Frowns for ever meet us.

Nixon Waterman

A warm smile thaws the icy stare.

Merv Rosell

If you would find greater joy in life, attempt to serve and please someone every day. The gift of yourself to someone who needs you will, in return, bring the gift of confidence and serenity to you.

John H. Crowe

Every cloud has a silver lining.

Unknown

They might not need me—yet they might—
I'll let my heart be just in sight—
A smile so small as mine might be
Precisely their necessity.

Emily Dickinson

True humor springs not more from the head than from the heart; it is not
contempt, its essence is love; it issues not in laughter, but in smiles,
which lie far deeper.

Thomas Carlyle

I'm a cheerful sort of man and very disposed to laughter. You wouldn't
believe . . . the number of things that strike me as being funny. I can
laugh at pretty nearly everything, I can.

Uncle Albert Wigg, in Mary Poppins, *P. L. Travers*

There is no duty we underrate so much as the duty of being happy.

Robert Louis Stevenson

You grow up the day you have your first real laugh—at yourself.

Unknown

Grin and bear it.

Unknown

What indescribable joy!—joy over God the Almighty. . . . For this is the absolute joy, to adore the almighty power with which God the Almighty bears all thy care and sorrow as easily as nothing.

Vernard Eller

Ignore dull days; forget the showers; Keep count of only shining hours.

Found on a sundial in Germany

It must be said that we can have joy, and therefore will have it, only as we give it to others.

Karl Barth

I wish you all the joy you can wish.

William Shakespeare

MOVING OUT

Growing Friendships

Office deadlines, career challenges, favorite hobbies—when all these things are gone we'll see that only people last forever. Your investment of yourself in the lives of other people is treasure laid up in heaven (see Matthew 6:20-21).

Friendship is like money, easier made than kept.

Samuel Butler

Our human relationships are the actual conditions in which the ideal life of God is to be exhibited.

Oswald Chambers, My Utmost for His Highest

A friend is a person who goes around saying nice things about you behind your back.

Unknown

Sympathy is two hearts tugging at the same load.

Carl S. Winters

We are born helpless. As soon as we are fully conscious, we discover loneliness. We need others physically, emotionally, intellectually; we need them if we are to know anything, even ourselves.

C. S. Lewis

We stand in the light of others, and that light reveals to us who we ourselves are.

Mike Mason

Two are better than one,
because they have a good return for their work:
If one falls down, his friend can help him up.
But pity the man who falls and has no one to help him up!

Ecclesiastes 4:9-10

Real friends are those who, when you've made a fool of yourself, don't feel that you've done a permanent job.

Anonymous

People with deep and lasting friendships may be introverts, extroverts, young, old, dull, intelligent, homely, good-looking; but the one characteristic they always have in common is openness. They have a certain transparency, allowing people to see what is in their hearts.

Alan Loy McGinnis, The Friendship Factor

When you help someone else up the hill, you reach the top yourself.

Anonymous

It is no small thing to be on terms of friendship with God.

Mrs. Charles E. Cowman, Streams in the Desert

The door to the human heart can be opened only from the inside.

Jo Petty, Apples of Gold

What a Friend we have in Jesus, all our sins and griefs to bear.
What a privilege to carry everything to God in prayer.

Joseph Scriven, "What a Friend We Have in Jesus"

There is a friend who sticks closer than a brother.

Proverbs 18:24

Friendship is to be purchased only by friendship.

Unknown

The best way to form a friendship is to become interested in other people, not by trying to interest people in you.

Dale Carnegie

The only way to have a friend is to be one.

Unknown

Here's to the friends that I love best,
  To those who have always stood the test;
To the friends I love who are tried and true,
  Friends that are old, and those that are new.
Life at its best to most is a trial,
  'Tis friendship that makes life really worthwhile.

E. K. Orr

A real friend is a person who walks in when everybody else walks out.

Unknown

A person is the single most limitless entity in creation, and if there is anything that is even more unlimited and unrestrained in its possibilities than is a person, then it is two people together.

Mike Mason

CHOOSE

The single clenched fist lifted and ready,
Or the open asking hand held out and waiting.
Choose:
For we meet by one or the other.

Carl Sandburg

Our restlessness within can only be met by the revelation of God's eternal friendship and love for us.

Margaret Bottome

No man has penned a truer line since the old world knew birth—
I wouldn't trade a friend of mine for all the gold on earth.

Luke McLuke

In each one of us the holiest and neediest and most sensitive place of all has been made and is reserved for God alone, so that only He can enter there. No one else can love us as He does, and no one else can be the sort of Friend to us that He is.

Mike Mason

May the hinges of friendship never grow rusty.

Unknown

How seldom we weigh our neighbor in the same balance with ourselves.

Thomas à Kempis

Friendship is the only cement that will ever hold the world together.

Jo Petty, Apples of Gold

A friend is a present you give yourself.

Robert Louis Stevenson

We're not primarily put on this earth to see through one another, but to see one another through.

Peter DeVries, Let Me Count the Ways

FRIENDSHIP

I've discovered a way to stay friends forever—
There's really nothing to it.
I simply tell you what to do
And you do it!

Shel Silverstein, A Light in the Attic

O Lord, in sorrow and in joy, open thou our lives to one another that we may live. Open thou our lives to thee that even in dying we may never die.

Frederick Buechner, The Hungering Dark

To get the full value of a joy, you must have somebody to divide it with.

Mark Twain

Intimacy, then, is always difficult, and when it stops being difficult it stops being intimacy.

Andrew Greeley

Becoming an expert at friendship will be one of the most rewarding projects of your lifetime.

Alan Loy McGinnis, The Friendship Factor

Some of the greatest men I have had the privilege of knowing not only are the most humble, but are those who express their humility by becoming actual servants in their relationships with others.

Mark O. Hatfield

Greater love has no one than this, that he lay down his life for his friends.

John 15:13

To be is to be vulnerable.

Norman O. Brown

Money can't buy friends but you get a better class of enemies.

Spike Milligan

Every life we touch is a field, everything we do and all the words we speak, are seed. What will the harvest be?

Rowland

The only way to get the best of an argument is to avoid it.

Dale Carnegie

We gain nothing by being with such as ourselves: we encourage each other in mediocrity. I am always longing to be with men more excellent than myself.

Charles Lamb

Do unto others as if you were the others.

Elbert Hubbard

If you approach each new person you meet in the spirit of adventure, you will find yourself endlessly fascinated by the new channels of thought and experience and personality that you encounter.

Eleanor Roosevelt

As iron sharpens iron,
so one man sharpens another.

Proverbs 27:17

Make new friends, but keep the old—
One is silver, and the other gold.

Children's song

A loyal friend laughs at your jokes when they're not so good, and sympathizes with your problems when they're not so bad.

Arnold H. Glasow

If a man be gracious to strangers, it shows that he is a citizen of the world, and his heart is no island, cut off from other islands, but a continent that joins them both.

Francis Bacon

A friend loves at all times.

Proverbs 17:17

There is no such thing as life apart from relationship . . . no life apart from the sharing of ourselves with another.

Mike Mason

Looking for Love

In a world where people fall in and out of love as often as they go to the movies, look for the source of real love. Get ready to love by learning to love God, who is Love itself.

The first duty of love is to listen.

Paul Tillich

My heart is a bargain today. Will you take it?

W. C. Fields

Respect is love in plain clothes.

Frankie Byrne

The supreme happiness of life is the conviction of being loved for yourself, or, more correctly, being loved in spite of yourself.

Victor Hugo

Love at first sight is a great time-saver.

Unknown

Love must be learned, and learned again and again; there is no end to it.
Hate needs no instruction, but wants only to be provoked.

Katherine Anne Porter

Love is a feeling to be learned.

Walter Trobisch

If music be the food of love, play on.

William Shakespeare, Twelfth Night

'Tis better to have loved and lost than never to have loved at all.

Alfred Lord Tennyson

'Tis better to have loved and lost—than just to have lost!

C. Stephen Board

True love is a gift on which no return is demanded. To love unselfishly is its own reward. To love for fulfillment, satisfaction, or pride is no love.

Og Mandino

Love asks for everything. Not just for a little bit, or a whole lot, but for everything. And unless one is challenged to give everything, one is not really in love.

Mike Mason, The Mystery of Marriage

But God demonstrates his own love for us in this: While we were still sinners, Christ died for us.

Romans 5:8

Love cannot be wasted. It makes no difference where it is bestowed, it always brings in big returns.

Unknown

True love is not a feeling by which we are overwhelmed. It is a committed, thoughtful decision.

M. Scott Peck, The Road Less Traveled

The arc of love from God to men
  orbiting, goes to him again.
My love, to loving God above,
  captures *me* in the round of love.

Luci Shaw, "Circles," Listen to the Green

Love one another. As I have loved you, so you must love one another.

John 13:34

Love without ceasing,
  Give without measure—
Who can exhaust
  God's limitless treasure?

Malcolm Schloss

To love at all is to be vulnerable. Love anything, and your heart will certainly be wrung and possibly broken. . . . The only place outside Heaven where you can be perfectly safe from all the dangers and perturbations of love is Hell.

C. S. Lewis, The Four Loves

The capacity to care is the thing which gives life its deepest significance.

Pablo Casals

unless you love someone nothing else makes any sense.

e.e. cummings

It is a long and hard road; it is an altar of sacrifice. . . . Love is the only way to our human destiny and to the feet of God, who is love.

John Powell, Why Am I Afraid to Love?

The most prevalent failure of Christian love is the failure to express it.

Rev. Paul E. Johnson, Christian Love

Love consists in this, that two solitudes protect and touch and greet each other.

Rainer Maria Rilke

Love must be tough.

James Dobson

Love is the medicine for the sickness of mankind. We can live if we have love.

Karl Menninger

Love is like quicksilver in the hand. Leave the fingers open and it stays. Clutch it, and it darts away.

Dorothy Parker

I like not only to be loved, but also to be told that I am loved.

George Eliot

To love, and be loved, is the greatest happiness of existence.

Sydney Smith

Adam invented love at first sight, one of the greatest labor-saving devices the world ever saw.

Josh Billings

The risk of love
is that of being unreturned.

Luci Shaw, "Perfect love banishes fear," Listen to the Green

Love your enemy—it'll drive him nuts.

Unknown

Love brings people out into the light. . . . Love aims at revelation, at a clarifying and defining of our true natures. It is a sort of sharpening process, a paring away of dull and lifeless exteriors so that the keen new edge of a person's new self can begin to flash and gleam in the light of day.

Mike Mason, The Mystery of Marriage

Love never fails.

1 Corinthians 13:8

Love is never afraid of giving too much.

Unknown

If we empty our hearts of self, God will fill them with his love.

Charles H. Spurgeon

Building Character

Graduation is a time of change, and all change points are crucial times for setting personal goals and establishing personal habits. Give some time and attention to the way you are "working out" and "shaping up" on the inside.

Everybody thinks of changing humanity, and nobody thinks of changing himself.

Leo Tolstoy

Happiness is not the end of life: character is.

Henry Ward Beecher, "Life Thoughts"

Make it your ambition to lead a quiet life, to mind your own business and to work with your hands, just as we told you, so that your daily life may win the respect of outsiders and so that you will not be dependent on anybody.

1 Thessalonians 4:11-12

Reputation is what men and women think of us. Character is what God and angels know of us.

Thomas Paine

A good name is more desirable than great riches;
to be esteemed is better than silver or gold.

Proverbs 22:1

You are redeemed to be set aside for God's special use and made a partaker of his moral perfection.

John White, The Fight

The joy of heaven begins as soon as we attain the character of heaven.
Keith L. Brooks, The Cream Book: Sentence Sermons

Character is like the foundation to a house . . . it is below the surface.
Unknown

Self-discipline is usually love, translated into action.
M. Scott Peck, The Road Less Traveled

Initiative is doing the right thing without being told.

Elbert Hubbard

The highest reward for a man's toil is not what he gets for it, but rather what he becomes by it.

Jo Petty, Apples of Gold

Christian character is not an inheritance; each individual must build it for himself.

Unknown

A moment's insight is sometimes worth a life's experience.

Oliver W. Holmes

Greatness is a two-faced coin—and its reverse is humility.

Unknown

If I take care of my character, my reputation will take care of itself.

Dwight L. Moody

A good name keeps its lustre in the dark.

John Ray

Let love and faithfulness never leave you;
bind them around your neck,
write them on the tablet of your heart.
Then you will win favor and a good name
in the sight of God and man.

Proverbs 3:3-4

I look upon the sublime and childish virtues of veracity and honesty as
the root of all that is sublime in character.

Ralph Waldo Emerson

Be at war with your vices, at peace with your neighbors, and let every
new year find you a better man.

Benjamin Franklin

Occasions do not make a man either strong or weak, but they show what
he is.

Thomas à Kempis

Character is like a tree and reputation like its shadow. The shadow is what we think of it; the tree is the real thing.

Abraham Lincoln

Character is best formed in the stormy billows of the world.

Goethe

I hope I shall possess firmness and virtue enough to maintain what I consider the most enviable of all titles, that of an "honest man."

George Washington

Sometimes when I get up in the morning . . . I feel like I've just got to bite a cat! I feel like if I don't bite a cat before sundown, I'll go crazy! But then I just take a deep breath and forget about it. That's what's known as real maturity.

Snoopy (Peanuts)

God's preparing His heroes; and when opportunity comes, He can fit them into their place in a moment, and the world will wonder where they came from.

A. B. Simpson

Holiness is not only expected, it is the promised birthright of every Christian. . . . To be holy is to be morally blameless. It is to be separated from sin and, therefore, consecrated to God.

Jerry Bridges, The Pursuit of Holiness

The man who masters himself is free.

Epictetus

He who reigns within himself, and rules passions, desires, and fears, is more than a king.

John Milton

Character is much easier kept than recovered.

Thomas Paine

Character is what you are in the dark.

Dwight L. Moody

Character in matters great and small consists in a man steadily pursuing the things of which he feels himself capable.

Unknown

The only reputation that matters is your reputation in heaven.

Keith L. Brooks, The Cream Book: Sentence Sermons

The measure of a man's real character is what he would do if he knew he would never be found out.

Thomas Macauley

Our acts make or mar us—we are the children of our own deeds.

Victor Hugo

Try not to become a man of success, but rather try to become a man of value.

Albert Einstein

Make yourself an honest man and then you may be sure there is one less rascal in the world.

Thomas Carlyle

A peace above all earthly dignities, a still and quiet conscience.

William Shakespeare

He has showed you, O man, what is good. And what does the LORD require of you? To act justly and to love mercy and to walk humbly with your God.

Micah 6:8

No man doth safely rule but he that hath learned gladly to obey.

Thomas à Kempis, The Imitation of Christ

When our vision of God is one of a God of relentless tenderness, we ultimately become tender ourselves.

Brennan Manning

Humility is to make a right estimate of oneself.

Charles H. Spurgeon

It is not by a man's purse, but by his character, that he is rich or poor.

Robert Louis Stevenson

Fear God and keep his commandments,
for this is the whole duty of man.

Ecclesiastes 12:13

No legacy is so rich as honesty.

William Shakespeare

Blessed are the pure in heart, for they will see God.

Matthew 5:8

There's no heavier burden than great potential.

Linus (Peanuts)

To go on being filled with the Spirit is to grow in holiness continually.

John White, The Fight

To thine own self be true.

William Shakespeare

Modesty is the art of encouraging people to find out for themselves how wonderful you are.

Unknown

You better not compromise yourself. It's all you got.

Janis Joplin

Integrity means an uncompromising adherence to a code of moral values: utter sincerity, honesty, and candor. It is an absence of deception, expediency, artificiality, or shallowness of any kind.

John Souter

Self-discipline is when your conscience tells you to do something and you don't talk back.

W. K. Hope

Joy is found in obedience.

Richard Foster, The Celebration of Discipline

Maturity is the capacity to endure uncertainty.

John Finley

Bad habits are like a comfortable bed—easy to get into, but hard to get out of.

Unknown

A Christian is a person who makes you think of Jesus.

Robert C. Savage, Pocket Quips

True repentance empties the soul of sin, separates the self from sin, and sets us free to follow God, to live rightly, wholesomely, as we were meant to live.

David Augsburger, The Freedom of Forgiveness

The person who has the approval of his own conscience has a powerful ally.

Unknown

He who most clearly discerns the perfect character of Jesus will be most urgent in prayer for grace to be like him.

Charles H. Spurgeon

Talent is nurtured in solitude; character is formed in the stormy billows of the world.

Goethe

A good name is better than fine perfume.

Ecclesiastes 7:1

Great Expectations

The future stretches out before you, like a white canvas ready to be painted with the bright colors of your life. Don't fear the days to come, but look forward in faith and anticipate the blessings God has for you right around the corner.

The future is as bright as the promises of God. We know not what the future holds, but we know who holds the future.

Robert C. Savage, Pocket Quips

Here's to your future,
   Your present and your past.
May each new day
   Be happier than the last.

Unknown

The future is a convenient place for dreams.

Anatole France

For the Son of Man is going to come in his Father's glory with his angels, and then he will reward each person according to what he has done.

Matthew 16:27

Let yesterday trouble you unduly today and you will ruin tomorrow.

Unknown

Hitch your wagon to a star.

Ralph Waldo Emerson

God is down in front. He is in the tomorrows. It is tomorrow that fills men with dread. God is there already.

F. B. Meyer

Where will I be five years from now? I delight in not knowing. That's one of the greatest things about life—its wonderful surprises.

Marlo Thomas

Our Lord holds His most vital and best things in store for those who mean business, for those who hunger and thirst for His very best.

Miles J. Stanford, Principles of Spiritual Growth

I am willing to go anywhere provided it be forward.

David Livingstone

Soon He's coming back to welcome me
Far beyond the starry sky;
I shall wing my flight to worlds unknown,
I shall reign with Him on high.

Luther Bridgers, "There's Within My Heart a Melody"

I've developed a new philosophy. . . . I only dread one day at a time.

Charlie Brown (Peanuts)

The present moment more resembles eternity than any other, because in it the present, the past, and the future converge.

Eugene Peterson, Traveling Light

Get excited about your home in heaven with God—it will change the way you live each day here on earth while you wait for the day you'll be home forever.

Annette Heinrich, One in a Zillion

Aim at heaven and you will get earth thrown in. Aim at earth and you will get neither.

C. S. Lewis, Mere Christianity

The same everlasting Father who cares for you today will take care of you tomorrow, and every day.

Frances de Sales

The future is that period of time in which our affairs prosper, our friends are true, and our happiness is assured.

Ambrose Bierce

When Christ shall come with shout of acclamation,
and take me home, what joy shall fill my heart.
Then I shall bow in humble adoration,
And there proclaim, "My God, how great Thou art!"

Stuart K. Hine, "How Great Thou Art"

You can't start worrying about what's going to happen. You get spastic enough worrying about what's happening now.

Lauren Bacall

Forgetting what is behind and straining toward what is ahead, I press on toward the goal to win the prize for which God has called me heavenward in Christ Jesus.

Philippians 3:13-14

The only limit to our realization of tomorrow will be our doubts of today.

Franklin D. Roosevelt

Listen, I tell you a mystery: We will not all sleep, but we will all be changed—in a flash, in the twinkling of an eye, at the last trumpet. For the trumpet will sound, the dead will be raised imperishable, and we will be changed.

1 Corinthians 15:51-52

You better live your best and act your best and think your best today; for today is the sure preparation for tomorrow and all the other tomorrows that follow.

Harriet Martineau

Whatever the Lord takes in hand He will accomplish; hence past mercies are guarantees for the future and admirable reasons for continuing to cry unto Him.

Charles H. Spurgeon

The pace of events is moving so fast that unless we can find some way to keep our sights on tomorrow, we cannot expect to be in touch with today.

Dean Rusk

What lies behind us and what lies before us are tiny matters compared to what lies within us.

Ralph Waldo Emerson

My interest is in the future because I am going to spend the rest of my life there.

Charles F. Kettering

Perhaps the best thing about the future is that it only comes one day at a time.

Dean Acheson

Life with Christ is an endless hope; without him a hopeless end.

Merv Rosell, Driftwood

I never think of the future—it comes soon enough.

Albert Einstein

We must see to it that enthusiasm for the future does not give rise to contempt for the past.

Pope Paul VI

He who provides for this life, but takes no care for eternity, is wise for a moment, but a fool forever.

Tillotson

In my Father's house are many rooms; if it were not so, I would have told you. I am going there to prepare a place for you. And if I go and prepare a place for you, I will come back and take you to be with me that you also may be where I am.

John 14:2-3